The
GREEN
THOREAU

The
GREEN
THOREAU

*America's First Environmentalist
on Technology, Possessions,
Livelihood, and More*

REVISED EDITION

Selected and with an Introduction
by Carol Spenard LaRusso

New World Library
Novato, California

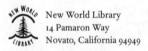

New World Library
14 Pamaron Way
Novato, California 94949

Copyright © 1992, 2012 by Carol LaRusso

Text design by Tona Pearce Myers

Library of Congress Cataloging-in-Publication Data
Thoreau, Henry David, 1817–1862.
 The green Thoreau : America's first environmentalist on technology, possessions, livelihood, and more / Henry David Thoreau ; selected and with an introduction by Carol Spenard LaRusso. — Rev. ed.
    p.   cm.
Includes bibliographical references.
ISBN 978-1-60868-143-3 (pbk. : acid-free paper)
1. Thoreau, Henry David, 1817-1862—Quotations. 2. Nature—Quotations, maxims, etc. 3. Conduct of life—Quotations, maxims, etc. 4. Technology in literature. 5. Nature conservation in literature. I. LaRusso, Carol Spenard, 1935– II. Title.
PS3042.L37 2012
818'.402—dc23   2012019557

First printing of revised edition, September 2012
ISBN 978-1-60868-143-3
Printed in Canada on 100% postconsumer-waste recycled paper

New World Library is proud to be a Gold Certified Environmentally Responsible Publisher. Publisher certification awarded by Green Press Initiative. www.greenpressinitiative.org

10 9 8 7 6 5 4 3 2 1

*For my children and grandchildren
and all young life on our planet*

CONTENTS

INTRODUCTION

Thoreau: A Man for the Twenty-First Century

The words of Henry David Thoreau (1817–1862) sound with a deep resonance in the opening decades of the twenty-first century. One hundred and fifty years after his death, the clarity of his vision seems marked especially for our time. Thoreau, with his deep love of the natural world, used nature as his teacher and companion, and as a source of healing, renewal, and inspiration.

Though Thoreau's writings and message were largely ignored during his lifetime and afterward as well, we no longer have the luxury of time in which to be similarly shortsighted. We are among the first generations to experience the effects of exponential population explosion, rampant industrialism, myriad technological inventions, dizzying social-political change, and climatic and environmental damage — all of which have dramatically altered our familiar planetary landscape within a few short decades.

Thoreau, probably the first environmentalist (long before that concept was ever formed), divined that "in wildness is the preservation of the world." These prophetic words serve as our wake-up call. Only recently we've learned how the systematic destruction of the rain forest has adversely affected the ecosystem of our fragile planet. In the face of many environmental and ethical difficulties we look around us for help. Not only do we need brilliant new technology created, but we also need inspiration, vision, and guidance. In Thoreau's always eloquent and often lyrical prose, we find a nineteenth-century man so amazingly ahead of his time that most of us in the twenty-first century have not yet caught up. He has much to teach us about not only the nurturing of our natural world but also the wise management of all our resources: our time, money, work, talents, health.

Thoreau believed in the freedom and potential of the individual, that each of us makes a difference in influencing our collective human life. Despite the power and proliferation of world governments, we have seen over and over again the incredible power of the individual and of the people — of grassroots movements that shape history. One of the most famous was influenced by Thoreau's essay "On the Duty of Civil Disobedience," which served as the primer for Gandhi's nonviolent resistance campaign in India. The civil rights movement led by Martin Luther King Jr. was similarly influenced. Even the "second" Russian revolution in the Soviet Union in 1991 demonstrated the concept of passive resistance to an unjust government. Thoreau was not an especially political man but was a man of courage who definitely "walked his talk." In 1846 he spent a night in the Concord, Massachusetts, jail for refusing to pay a poll tax to a government that supported slavery and the Mexican War.

But Thoreau, a freedom-loving individualist, would not want us to imitate him. Rather, he demands that we examine how we spend our lives and then work out our own salvation. Thoreau chose to build a cabin on the shores of Walden Pond and live there for over two years, not to escape society or to set an example but to learn his life lessons: "I went to the woods because I wished to live deliberately, to front only the essential facts of life, and see if I could not learn what it had to teach." Each of us will learn our life lessons in our own way — finding our own personal "Walden."

Our path ahead as citizens and custodians of planet Earth may be difficult. It could be that we must downshift and make some sacrifices in order to achieve other, more important goals. Much of what Thoreau says is not what we want to hear. He asks, "Shall we always study to obtain more of these things [possessions], and not sometimes be content with less?" and reminds us, "A man is rich in proportion to the number of things he can afford to let alone." Thoreau's compelling observations serve as catalysts for us to rethink our lives and discover how to live them with more integrity and wisdom. We could wander in the treasure trove of his thought indefinitely.

The Green Thoreau has been prepared as both a practical and an inspirational guide for our way forward in these tumultuous times. I have selected illustrative passages from Thoreau's lesser-known essays and books (some of which were delivered as lectures and published posthumously), as well as from *Walden*, published in 1854. His artistry, passion, and vision inspire us to reach beyond our years and experience to more wisely face the challenges of this new millennium. Thoreau is there already — our best guide and teacher.

A note on the text: We can interpret Thoreau's use of the words *man* and *men* to include women as well! Some outdated punctuation has been changed to reflect modern usage; for example, where a dash was preceded by a comma, the comma has been omitted, and obsolete hyphens have been eliminated from such words as *to-day* and *to-morrow*. However, no changes have been made that would alter Thoreau's meaning or thought.

— *Carol Spenard LaRusso*

The
GREEN
THOREAU

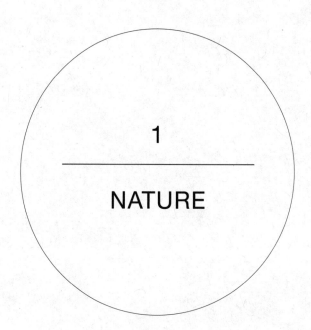

1

NATURE

The earth is not a mere fragment of dead history, stratum upon stratum like the leaves of a book, to be studied by geologists and antiquaries chiefly, but living poetry like the leaves of a tree, which precede flowers and fruit — not a fossil earth, but a living earth.

Walden,
SPRING

This winter they are cutting down our woods more seriously than ever.... Thank God, they cannot cut down the clouds!

Journal,
JANUARY 21, 1852

If a man walks in the woods for love of them half of each day, he is in danger of being regarded as a loafer; but if he spends his whole day as a speculator, shearing off those woods and making earth bald before her time, he is esteemed an industrious and enterprising citizen. As if a town had no interest in its forests but to cut them down!

Life Without Principle

I wish to speak a word for Nature, for absolute freedom and wildness, as contrasted with a freedom and culture merely civil — to regard man as an inhabitant, or a part and parcel of Nature, rather than a member of society.

Walking

Nowadays almost all man's improvements, so called, as the building of houses and the cutting down of the forest and of all large trees, simply deform the landscape, and make it more and more tame and cheap.

Walking

He who cuts down woods beyond a certain limit exterminates birds.

Journal,
MAY 17, 1853

When I consider that the nobler animals have been exterminated here — the cougar, panther, lynx, wolverine, wolf, bear, moose, deer, the beaver, the turkey, etc., etc. — I cannot but feel as if I lived in a tamed, and, as it were, emasculated country.

Journal,
MARCH 23, 1856

Our village life would stagnate if it were not for the unexplored forests and meadows which surround it. We need the tonic of wildness — to wade sometimes in marshes where the bittern and the meadow-hen lurk, and hear the booming of the snipe; to smell the whispering sedge where only some wilder and more solitary fowl builds her nest, and the mink crawls with its belly close to the ground.

Walden,
SPRING

Each town should have a park, or rather a primitive forest, of five hundred or a thousand acres, where a stick should never be cut for fuel, a common possession forever, for instruction and recreation.

Journal,
OCTOBER 15, 1859

Most men, it seems to me, do not care for Nature and would sell their share in all her beauty, as long as they may live, for a stated sum — many for a glass of rum. Thank God, men cannot as yet fly, and lay waste the sky as well as the earth! We are safe on that side for the present. It is for the very reason that some do not care for those things that we need to continue to protect all from the vandalism of a few.

Journal,
JANUARY 3, 1861

The era of the Wild Apple will soon be past. It is a fruit which will probably become extinct in New England....I fear that he who walks over these fields a century hence will not know the pleasure of knocking

off wild apples. Ah, poor man, there are many pleasures which he will not know!

Wild Apples

There is a higher law affecting our relation to pines as
well as to men. A pine cut down, a dead pine, is no more
a pine than a dead human carcass is a man. Can he who
has discovered only some of the values of whalebone
and whale oil be said to have discovered the true use
of the whale? Can he who slays the elephant for his
ivory be said to have "seen the elephant"?... Every
creature is better alive than dead, men and moose
and pine-trees, and he who understands it aright will
rather preserve its life than destroy it....

The very willow-rows lopped every three years
for fuel and powder, and every sizable pine or oak,
or other forest tree, cut down within the memory of
man! As if individual speculators were to be allowed
to export the clouds out of the sky, or the stars out of
the firmament, one by one.

The Maine Woods,
CHESUNCOOK

It concerns us all whether these proprietors choose to cut down all the woods this winter or not.

Journal,
JANUARY 22, 1852

They have cut down two or three of the very rare celtis trees, not found anywhere else in town. The Lord deliver us from these vandalic proprietors!...

If some are prosecuted for abusing children, others deserve to be prosecuted for maltreating the face of nature committed to their care.

Journal,
SEPTEMBER 28, 1857

What is the use of a house if you haven't got a tolerable planet to put it on?

Familiar Letters, THOREAU TO HARRISON BLAKE,
MAY 20, 1860

At the same time that we are earnest to explore and learn all things, we require that all things be mysterious and unexplorable, that land and sea be infinitely wild, unsurveyed and unfathomed by us because unfathomable. We can never have enough of Nature.

Walden,
SPRING

The seashore is a sort of neutral ground, a most advantageous point from which to contemplate this world .... The waves forever rolling to the land are too far-traveled and untamable to be familiar....

Though once there were more whales cast up here, I think that it was never more wild than now. We do not associate the idea of antiquity with the ocean, nor wonder how it looked a thousand years ago, as we do of the land, for it was equally wild and unfathomable always.... The aspect of the shore only has changed. The ocean is a wilderness reaching round the globe.... Serpents, bears, hyenas, tigers, rapidly vanish as civilization advances, but the most populous and civilized city cannot scare a shark far from its wharves.

Cape Cod,
THE SEA AND THE DESERT

In Wildness is the preservation of the World....Life consists with wildness. The most alive is the wildest.

Walking

"Nothing that naturally happens to man can *hurt* him, earthquakes and thunderstorms not excepted," said a man of genius, who at this time lived a few miles farther on our road. When compelled by a shower to take shelter under a tree, we may improve that opportunity for a more minute inspection of some of Nature's works. I have stood under a tree in the woods half a day at a time, during a heavy rain in the summer, and yet employed myself happily and profitably there prying with microscopic eye into the crevices of the bark or the leaves of the fungi at my feet.

A Week on the Concord and Merrimack Rivers,
THURSDAY

What is it that makes it so hard sometimes to determine whither we will walk? I believe that there is a subtle magnetism in Nature, which, if we unconsciously yield to it, will direct us aright. It is not indifferent to us which way we walk. There is a right way; but we are very liable from heedlessness and stupidity to take the wrong one. We would fain take that walk, never yet taken by us through this actual world, which is perfectly symbolical of the path which we love to travel in the interior and ideal world; and sometimes, no doubt, we find it difficult to choose our direction, because it does not yet exist distinctly in our idea.

Walking

The West of which I speak is but another name for the Wild; and what I have been preparing to say is, that in Wildness is the preservation of the World. Every tree sends its fibers forth in search of the Wild. The cities import it at any price. Men plow and sail for it. From the forest and wilderness come the tonics and barks which brace mankind. Our ancestors were savages. The story of Romulus and Remus being suckled by a wolf is not a meaningless fable. The founders of every state which has risen to eminence have drawn their nourishment and vigor from a similar wild source. It was because the children of the Empire were not suckled by the wolf that they were conquered and displaced by the children of the northern forests who were.

Walking

For my part, I feel that with regard to Nature I live a sort of border life, on the confines of a world into which I make occasional and transient forays only, and my patriotism and allegiance to the state into whose territories I seem to retreat are those of a moss-trooper. Unto a life which I call natural I would gladly follow even a will-o'-the-wisp through bogs and sloughs unimaginable, but no moon nor firefly has shown me the causeway to it. Nature is a personality so vast and universal that we have never seen one of her features. The walker in the familiar fields which stretch around my native town sometimes finds himself in another land than is described in their owners' deeds, as it were in some faraway field on the confines of the actual Concord, where her jurisdiction ceases, and the idea which the word *Concord* suggests ceases to be suggested. These farms which I have myself surveyed, these bounds which I have set up, appear dimly still as through a mist; but they have no chemistry to fix them; they fade from the surface of the glass, and the picture which the painter painted stands out dimly from beneath. The world with which we are commonly acquainted leaves no trace, and it will have no anniversary.

Walking

I seek acquaintance with Nature — to know her moods and manners. Primitive Nature is the most interesting to me. I take infinite pains to know all the phenomena of the spring, for instance, thinking that I have here the entire poem, and then, to my chagrin, I hear that it is but an imperfect copy that I possess and have read, that my ancestors have torn out many of the first leaves and grandest passages, and mutilated it in many places. I should not like to think that some demigod had come before me and picked out some of the best of the stars. I wish to know an entire heaven and an entire earth.

Journal,
MARCH 23, 1856

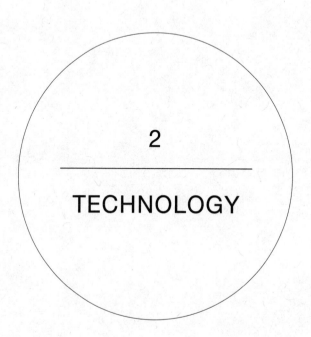

2

TECHNOLOGY

Men have become the tools of their tools.

Walden,
ECONOMY

The improvements of ages have had but little influence on the essential laws of man's existence; as our skeletons, probably, are not to be distinguished from those of our ancestors....

Our inventions are wont to be pretty toys, which distract our attention from serious things. They are but improved means to an unimproved end, an end which it was already but too easy to arrive at; as railroads lead to Boston or New York.

Walden,
ECONOMY

The nation itself, with all its so-called internal improvements, which, by the way, are all external and superficial, is...an unwieldy and overgrown establishment, cluttered with furniture and tripped up by its own traps, ruined by luxury and heedless expense, by want of calculation and a worthy aim, as the million households in the land; and the only cure for it as for them is in rigid economy, a stern and more than Spartan simplicity of life and elevation of purpose. It lives too fast. Men think that it is essential that the *Nation* have commerce, and export ice, and talk through a telegraph, and ride thirty miles an hour, without a doubt, whether *they* do or not; but whether we should live like baboons or like men, is a little uncertain.... We do not ride upon the railroad; it rides upon us.

Walden,
WHERE I LIVED, AND WHAT I LIVED FOR

We are in great haste to construct a magnetic telegraph from Maine to Texas; but Maine and Texas, it may be, have nothing important to communicate.... We are eager to tunnel under the Atlantic and bring the old world some weeks nearer to the new; but perchance the first news that will leak through into the broad, flapping American ear will be that the Princess Adelaide has the whooping cough.

Walden,
ECONOMY

Only make something to take the place of something, and men will behave as if it was the very thing they wanted.

A Week on the Concord and Merrimack Rivers,
MONDAY

Almost all our improvements, so called, tend to convert the country into the town.

Journal,
AUGUST 22, 1860

While civilization has been improving our houses, it has not equally improved the men who are to inhabit them. It has created palaces, but it was not so easy to create noblemen and kings.

Walden,
ECONOMY

We have heard of a Society for the Diffusion of Useful Knowledge. It is said that knowledge is power, and the like. Methinks there is equal need of a Society for the Diffusion of Useful Ignorance, what we will call Beautiful Knowledge, a knowledge useful in a higher sense: for what is most of our boasted so-called knowledge but a conceit that we know something, which robs us of the advantage of our actual ignorance? What we call knowledge is often our positive ignorance; ignorance our negative knowledge. By long years of patient industry and reading of the newspapers — for what are the libraries of science but files of newspapers — a man accumulates a myriad facts, lays them up in his memory, and then when in some spring of his life he saunters abroad into the Great Fields of thought, he, as it were, goes to grass like a horse and leaves all his harness behind in the stable. I would say to the Society for the Diffusion of Useful Knowledge, sometimes, Go to grass. You have eaten hay long enough.

Walking

How little do the most wonderful inventions of modern times detain us. They insult nature. Every machine, or particular application, seems a slight outrage against universal laws. How many fine inventions are there which do not clutter the ground? We think that those only succeed which minister to our sensible and animal wants, which bake or brew, wash or warm, or the like. But are those of no account which are patented by fancy and imagination, and succeed so admirably in our dreams that they give the tone still to our waking thoughts? Already nature is serving all those uses which science slowly derives on a much higher and grander scale to him that will be served by her. When the sunshine falls on the path of the poet, he enjoys all those pure benefits and pleasures which the arts slowly and partially realize from age to age. The winds which fan his cheek waft him the sum of that profit and happiness which their lagging inventions supply.

Paradise (to Be) Regained

There are the powers, too, of the Tide and Waves, constantly ebbing and flowing, lapsing and relapsing, but they serve man in but few ways. They turn a few tide-mills, and perform a few other insignificant and accidental services only. We all perceive the effect of the tide; how imperceptibly it creeps up into our harbors and rivers, and raises the heaviest navies as easily as the lightest chip. Everything that floats must yield to it. But man, slow to take nature's constant hint of assistance, makes slight and irregular use of this power, in careening ships and getting them afloat when aground....

This power may be applied in various ways. A large body, of the heaviest materials that will float, may first be raised by it, and being attached to the end of a balance reaching from the land, or from a stationary support fastened to the bottom, when the tide falls the whole weight will be brought to bear upon the end of the balance. Also, when the tide rises, it may be made to exert a nearly equal force in the opposite direction.

Paradise (to Be) Regained

Finally, there is the power to be derived from Sunshine, by the principle on which Archimedes contrived his burning-mirrors, a multiplication of mirrors reflecting the rays of the sun upon the same spot, till the requisite degree of heat is obtained. The principal application of this power will be to the boiling of water and production of steam. So much for these few and more obvious powers, already used to a trifling extent. But there are innumerable others in nature, not described nor discovered. These, however, will do for the present. This would be to make the sun and the moon equally our satellites. For, as the moon is the cause of the tides, and the sun the cause of the wind, which, in turn, is the cause of the waves, all the work of this planet would be performed by these far influences.

Paradise (to Be) Regained

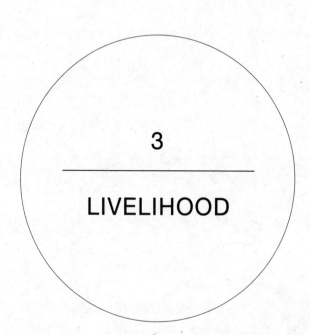

3

LIVELIHOOD

It is remarkable that there is little or nothing to be remembered written on the subject of getting a living; how to make getting a living not merely honest and honorable, but altogether inviting and glorious; for if getting a living is not so, then living is not.

Life Without Principle

I have travelled a good deal in Concord; and everywhere, in shops, and offices, and fields, the inhabitants have appeared to me to be doing penance in a thousand remarkable ways.... The twelve labors of Hercules were trifling in comparison with those which my neighbors have undertaken; for they were only twelve, and had an end; but I could never see that these men slew or captured any monster or finished any labor.... Actually, the laboring man has not leisure for a true integrity day by day; he cannot afford to sustain the manliest relations to men; his labor would be depreciated in the market. He has no time to be anything but a machine. How can he remember well his ignorance — which his growth requires — who has so often to use his knowledge?

Walden,
Economy

I have no doubt that some of you who read this book are unable to pay for all the dinners which you have actually eaten, or for the coats and shoes which are fast wearing or are already worn out, and have come to this page to spend borrowed or stolen time, robbing your creditors of an hour...always on the limits, trying to get into business and trying to get out of debt.

Walden,
Economy

Let not to get a living be thy trade, but thy sport. Enjoy the land, but own it not. Through want of enterprise and faith men are where they are, buying and selling, and spending their lives like serfs.

Walden,
BAKER FARM

It is hard to have a southern overseer; it is worse to have a northern one; but worst of all when you are the slave-driver of yourself.

Walden,
ECONOMY

Let us consider the way in which we spend our lives. This world is a place of business. What an infinite bustle! I am awaked almost every night by the panting of the locomotive. It interrupts my dreams. There is no Sabbath. It would be glorious to see mankind at leisure for once. It is nothing but work, work, work....

To have done anything by which you earned money *merely* is to have been truly idle or worse.... The aim of the laborer should be, not to get his living, to get "a good job," but to perform well a certain work; and, even in a pecuniary sense, it would be economy for a town to pay its laborers so well that they would not feel that they were working for low ends, as for a livelihood merely, but for scientific, or even moral ends. Do not hire a man who does your work for money, but him who does it for love of it....

There is no more fatal blunderer than he who consumes the greater part of this life getting his living. All great enterprises are self-supporting; the poet, for instance, must sustain his body by his poetry, as a steam planing-mill feeds its boilers with the shavings it makes. You must get your living by loving.

Life Without Principle

For more than five years I maintained myself thus solely by the labor of my hands, and I found that by working about six weeks in a year, I could meet all the expenses of living.

Walden,
ECONOMY

If I should sell both my forenoons and afternoons to society, as most appear to do, I am sure that for me there would be nothing left worth living for. I trust that I shall never thus sell my birthright for a mess of pottage. I wish to suggest that a man may be very industrious, and yet not spend his time well....

The ways in which most men get their living, that is, live, are mere makeshifts, and a shirking of the real business of life — chiefly because they do not know, but partly because they do not mean, any better.

Life Without Principle

The life which men praise and regard as successful is but one kind. Why should we exaggerate any one kind at the expense of the others?

It is not necessary that a man should earn his living by the sweat of his brow, unless he sweats easier than I do....

Walden,
ECONOMY

I would not subtract anything from the praise that is due to philanthropy, but merely demand justice for all who by their lives and works are a blessing to mankind.

I do not value chiefly a man's uprightness and benevolence, which are, as it were, his stem and leaves. Those plants of whose greenness withered we make herb tea for the sick, serve but a humble use, and are most employed by quacks. I want the flower and fruit of a man; that some fragrance be wafted over from him to me, and some ripeness flavor our intercourse.

Walden,
ECONOMY

There are certain pursuits which, if not wholly poetic and true, do at least suggest a nobler and finer relation to nature than we know. The keeping of bees, for instance, is a very slight interference. It is like directing the sunbeams. All nations, from the remotest antiquity, have thus fingered nature.

Paradise (to Be) Regained

Most men, even in this comparatively free country, through mere ignorance and mistake, are so occupied with the factitious cares and superfluously coarse labors of life, that its finer fruits cannot be plucked by them. Their fingers, from excessive toil, are too clumsy and tremble too much for that. Actually, the laboring man has not leisure for a true integrity day by day; he cannot afford to sustain the manliest relations to men; his labor would be depreciated in the market. He has no time to be any thing but a machine.

Walden,
Economy

4

LIVING

I went to the woods because I wished to live deliberately, to front only the essential facts of life, and see if
I could not learn what it had to teach, and not, when I
came to die, discover that I had not lived.

Walden,

<small>WHERE I LIVED, AND WHAT I LIVED FOR</small>

One young man of my acquaintance, who has inher-
ited some acres, told me that he thought he should live
as I did, *if he had the means.* I would not have anyone
adopt my mode of living on any account; for, besides
that before he has fairly learned it I may have found
out another for myself, I desire that there may be as
many different persons in the world as possible; but

I would have each one be very careful to find out and pursue his own way, and not his father's or his mother's or his neighbor's instead.

Walden,
ECONOMY

A man cannot be said to succeed in this life who does not satisfy one friend.

Journal,
FEBRUARY 19, 1857

To affect the quality of the day, that is the highest of arts. Every man is tasked to make his life, even in its details, worthy of the contemplation of his most elevated and critical hour....

Our life is frittered away by detail.... Simplicity, simplicity, simplicity! I say, let your affairs be as two or three, and not a hundred or a thousand; instead of a million count half a dozen, and keep your accounts on your thumbnail.

Walden,
WHERE I LIVED, AND WHAT I LIVED FOR

The mass of men lead lives of quiet desperation. What is called resignation is confirmed desperation. From the desperate city you go into the desperate country, and have to console yourself with the bravery of minks and muskrats. A stereotyped but unconscious despair is concealed even under what are called the games and amusements of mankind. There is no play in them, for this comes after work. But it is a characteristic of wisdom not to do desperate things.

When we consider what, to use the words of the catechism, is the chief end of man, and what are the true necessaries and means of life, it appears as if men had deliberately chosen the common mode of living because they preferred it to any other. Yet they honestly think there is no choice left. But alert and healthy natures remember that the sun rose clear. It is never too late to give up your prejudices. No way of thinking or doing, however ancient, can be trusted without proof.

Walden,
ECONOMY

What is the pill which will keep us well, serene, contented?...For my panacea, instead of one of those quack vials of a mixture dipped from Acheron and the Dead Sea…let me have a draught of undiluted morning air. Morning air! If men will not drink of this at the fountainhead of the day, why, then, we must even bottle up some and sell it in the shops, for the benefit of those who have lost their subscription ticket to morning time in this world.

Walden,
SOLITUDE

I think that I cannot preserve my health and spirits, unless I spend four hours a day at least — and it is commonly more than that — sauntering through the woods and over the hills and fields, absolutely free from all worldly engagements. . . . The mechanics and shopkeepers stay in their shops not only all the fore-noon, but all the afternoon too, sitting with crossed legs, so many of them — as if the legs were made to sit upon, and not to stand or walk upon — I think that they deserve some credit for not having all committed suicide long ago. . . .

The walking of which I speak has nothing in it akin

to taking exercise, as it is called, as the sick take medicine at stated hours — as the swinging of dumbbells or chairs; but is itself the enterprise and adventure of the day. If you would get exercise, go in search of the springs of life. Think of a man's swinging dumbbells for his health, when those springs are bubbling up in far-off pastures unsought by him!...

Of course it is of no use to direct our steps to the woods, if they do not carry us thither. I am alarmed when it happens that I have walked a mile into the woods bodily, without getting there in spirit.

Walking

If you would know the flavor of huckleberries, ask the cowboy or the partridge. It is a vulgar error to suppose that you have tasted huckleberries who never plucked them.... The ambrosial and essential part of the fruit is lost with the bloom which is rubbed off in the market cart, and they become mere provender.

Walden,
THE PONDS

Why concern ourselves so much about our beans for seed, and not be concerned at all about a new generation of men?

Walden,
THE BEANFIELD

The subject of sex is a remarkable one, since, though its phenomena concern us so much, both directly and indirectly, and, sooner or later, it occupies the thoughts of all, yet all mankind, as it were, agree to be silent about it, at least the sexes commonly to one another. One of the most interesting of all human facts is veiled more completely than any mystery.

Familiar Letters,
THOREAU TO HARRISON BLAKE,
SEPTEMBER 1852

Let us settle ourselves, and work and wedge our feet downward through the mud and slush of opinion, and prejudice, and tradition, and delusion and appearance, that alluvion which covers the globe, through Paris

and London, through New York and Boston and Concord, through church and state, through poetry and
philosophy and religion, till we come to a hard bottom
and rocks in place, which we can call *reality*, and say,
This is, and no mistake.... Be it life or death, we crave
only reality.

Walden,
WHERE I LIVED, AND WHAT I LIVED FOR

What is a course of history, or philosophy, or poetry,
no matter how well selected, or the best society, or
the most admirable routine of life, compared with
the discipline of looking always at what is to be seen?
Will you be a reader, a student merely, or a seer? Read
your fate, see what is before you, and walk on into
futurity.

Walden,
SOUNDS

Why level downward to our dullest perception always,
and praise that as common sense? The commonest

sense is the sense of men asleep, which they express by snoring.

Walden,
CONCLUSION

We spend more on almost any article of bodily aliment [nourishment] or ailment than on our mental aliment. It is time that we had uncommon schools, that we did not leave off our education when we begin to be men and women.

Walden,
READING

What everybody echoes or in silence passes by as true today may turn out to be falsehood tomorrow, mere smoke of opinion.... What old people say you cannot do, you try and find that you can. Old deeds for old people, and new deeds for new.

Walden,
ECONOMY

The fate of the country...does not depend on what kind of paper you drop into the ballot-box once a year, but on what kind of man you drop from your chamber into the street every morning.

Slavery in Massachusetts

I think that we should be men first, and subjects afterward. It is not desirable to cultivate a respect for the law, so much as for the right.

On the Duty of Civil Disobedience

The law will never make men free; it is men who have got to make the law free. They are the lovers of law and order, who observe the law when the government breaks it.

Slavery in Massachusetts

I am convinced that if all men were to live simply as I then did, thieving and robbery would be unknown. These take place only in communities where some have got more than is sufficient while others have not enough.

Walden,
THE VILLAGE

I left the woods for as good a reason as I went there. Perhaps it seemed to me that I had several more lives to live, and could not spare any more time for that one.

Walden,
CONCLUSION

Measure your health by your sympathy with morning and spring. If there is no response in you to the awakening of nature — if the prospect of an early morning walk does not banish sleep, if the warble of the first bluebird does not thrill you — know that the morning and spring of your life are past. Thus may you feel your pulse.

Journal,
FEBRUARY 25, 1859

5

POSSESSIONS

A man is rich in proportion to the number of things he can afford to let alone.

Walden,
WHERE I LIVED, AND WHAT I LIVED FOR

It would be some advantage to live a primitive and frontier life, though in the midst of an outward civilization, if only to learn what are the gross necessaries of life and what methods have been taken to obtain them; or even to look over the old day-books of the merchants, to see what it was that men most commonly bought at the stores, what they stored, that is, what are the grossest groceries....

The necessaries of life for man in this climate may,

accurately enough, be distributed under the several heads of Food, Shelter, Clothing, and Fuel; for not till we have secured these are we prepared to entertain the true problems of life with freedom and a prospect of success.... By proper Shelter and Clothing we legitimately retain our own internal heat; but with an excess of these, or of Fuel, that is, with an external heat greater than our own internal, may not cookery properly be said to begin?...

When a man is warmed by the several modes which I have described, what does he want next? Surely not more warmth of the same kind, as more and richer food, larger and more splendid houses, finer and more abundant clothing, more numerous, incessant, and hotter fires, and the like....

Shall we always study to obtain more of these things, and not sometimes be content with less?

Walden,
ECONOMY

Do not trouble yourself much to get new things, whether clothes or friends. Turn the old; return to them. Things do not change; we change. Sell your clothes and keep your thoughts.

Walden,
CONCLUSION

No man ever stood the lower in my estimation for having a patch in his clothes; yet I am sure that there is greater anxiety, commonly, to have fashionable, or at least clean and unpatched, clothes than to have a sound conscience....Most behave as if...it would be easier for them to hobble to town with a broken leg than with a broken pantaloon.

I say, beware of all enterprises that require new clothes, and not rather a new wearer of clothes. If there is not a new man, how can the new clothes be made to fit? If you have any enterprise before you, try it in your old clothes.

Walden,
ECONOMY

In my experience I have found nothing so truly impoverishing as what is called wealth, i.e., the command of greater means than you had before possessed, though comparatively few and slight still, for you thus inevitably acquire a more expensive habit of living, and even the very same necessaries and comforts cost you more than they once did. Instead of gaining, you have lost some independence, and if your income should be suddenly lessened, you would find yourself poor, though possessed of the same means which once made you rich.

Journal,
JANUARY 20, 1856

And when the farmer has got his house, he may not be the richer but the poorer for it, and it be the house that has got him....

Most of the luxuries, and many of the so-called comforts, of life are not only not indispensable, but positive hindrances to the elevation of mankind. With respect to luxuries and comforts, the wisest have ever lived a more simple and meager life than the poor.

Walden,
ECONOMY

That man is the richest whose pleasures are the cheapest.

Journal,
MARCH 11, 1856

At present, in this vicinity, the best part of the land is not private property; the landscape is not owned, and the walker enjoys comparative freedom. But possibly the day will come when it will be partitioned off into so-called pleasure-grounds, in which a few will take a narrow and exclusive pleasure only — when fences shall be multiplied, and man-traps and other engines invented to confine men to the public road, and walking over the surface of God's earth shall be construed to mean trespassing on some gentleman's grounds. To enjoy a thing exclusively is commonly to exclude yourself from the true enjoyment of it. Let us improve our opportunities, then, before the evil days come.

Walking

The richest gifts we can bestow are the least marketable. We hate the kindness which we understand. A noble person confers no such gift as his whole confidence: none so exalts the giver and the receiver; it produces the truest gratitude. Perhaps it is only essential to friendship that some vital trust should have been reposed by the one in the other. I feel addressed and probed even to the remote parts of my being when one nobly shows, even in trivial things, an implicit faith in me. When such divine commodities are so near and cheap, how strange that it should have to be each day's discovery! A threat or a curse may be forgotten, but this mild trust translates me. I am no more of this earth; it acts dynamically; it changes my very substance. I cannot do what before I did. I cannot be what before I was. Other chains may be broken, but in the darkest night, in the remotest place, I trail this thread. Then things cannot *happen*. What if God were to confide in us for a moment! Should we not then be gods?

Familiar Letters,
THOREAU TO RALPH WALDO EMERSON,
FEBRUARY 12, 1843

What you call bareness and poverty is to me simplicity. God could not be unkind to me if he should try. I love the winter, with its imprisonment and its cold, for it compels the prisoner to try new fields and resources. I love to have the river closed up for a season and a pause put to my boating, to be obliged to get my boat in. I shall launch it again in the spring with so much more pleasure. This is an advantage in point of abstinence and moderation compared with the seaside boating, where the boat ever lies on the shore. I love best to have each thing in its season only, and enjoy doing without it at all other times. It is the greatest of all advantages to enjoy no advantage at all. I find it invariably true, the poorer I am, the richer I am. What you consider my disadvantage, I consider my advantage. While you are pleased to get knowledge and culture in many ways, I am delighted to think that I am getting rid of them. I have never got over my surprise that I should have been born into the most estimable place in all the world, and in the very nick of time, too.

Journal,
DECEMBER 5, 1856

The savage lives simply through ignorance and idleness or laziness, but the philosopher lives simply through wisdom.

Journal,
SEPTEMBER 1, 1853

To what end do I lead a simple life at all, pray? That I may teach others to simplify their lives — and so all our lives be simplified merely, like an algebraic formula? Or not, rather, that I may make use of the ground I have cleared, to live more worthily and profitably?

Familiar Letters, THOREAU TO HARRISON BLAKE,
SEPTEMBER 26, 1855

The rule is to carry as little as possible.

Journal,
JULY 22, 1857

Simplicity is the law of nature for men as well as for flowers.

Journal,
FEBRUARY 29, 1852

At a certain season of our life we are accustomed to consider every spot as the possible site of a house. I have thus surveyed the country on every side within a dozen miles of where I live. In imagination I have bought all the farms in succession, for all were to be bought, and I knew their price. I walked over each farmer's premises, tasted his wild apples, discoursed on husbandry with him, took his farm at his price, at any price, mortgaging it to him in my mind; even put a higher price on it, took everything but a deed of it — took his word for his deed, for I dearly love to talk — cultivated it, and him too to some extent, I trust, and withdrew when I had enjoyed it long enough, leaving him to carry it on. This experience entitled me to be regarded as a sort of real-estate broker by my friends.

Walden,
WHERE I LIVED, AND WHAT I LIVED FOR

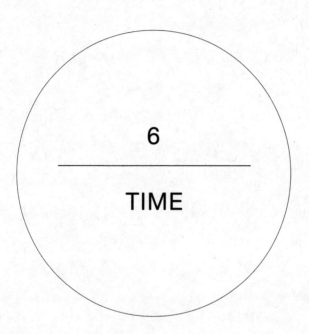

6

TIME

In any weather, at any hour of the day or night, I have been anxious to improve the nick of time, and notch it on my stick too; to stand on the meeting of two eternities, the past and future, which is precisely the present moment.

Walden,
ECONOMY

Why should we live with such hurry and waste of life? Let us spend one day as deliberately as Nature, and not be thrown off the track by every nutshell and mosquito's wing that falls on the rails....If the engine whistles, let it whistle till it is hoarse for its pains. If the bell rings, why should we run? ...

Walden,
WHERE I LIVED, AND WHAT I LIVED FOR

As if you could kill time without injuring eternity.

Walden,
ECONOMY

Many a forenoon have I stolen away, preferring to spend thus the most valued part of the day; for I was rich, if not in money, in sunny hours and summer days, and spent them lavishly.

Walden,
THE PONDS

I love a broad margin to my life. Sometimes, in a summer morning, having taken my accustomed bath, I sat in my sunny doorway from sunrise till noon, rapt in a revery, amidst the pines and hickories and sumacs, in undisturbed solitude and stillness. ... I grew in those seasons like corn in the night, and they were far better than any work of the hands would have been. They were not time subtracted from my life, but so much over and above my usual allowance....My days were not days of the week, bearing the stamp of any heathen deity, nor were they minced into hours and fretted by the ticking of a clock; for I lived like the Puri Indians, of whom it is said that "for yesterday, today, and tomorrow they have only one word, and they express the variety of meaning by pointing backward for yesterday, forward for tomorrow, and overhead for the passing day."

Walden,
SOUNDS

In eternity there is indeed something true and sublime. But all these times and places and occasions are now and here. God Himself culminates in the present moment, and will never be more divine in the lapse of all the ages.

Walden,
WHERE I LIVED, AND WHAT I LIVED FOR

We should be blessed if we lived in the present always, and took advantage of every accident that befell us... and did not spend our time in atoning for the neglect of past opportunities, which we call doing our duty. We loiter in winter while it is already spring.

Walden,
SPRING

The startings and arrivals of the [railway] cars...go and come with such regularity and precision, and their whistle can be heard so far, that the farmers set their clocks by them, and thus one well-conducted institution regulates a whole country. Have not men improved somewhat in punctuality since the railroad was invented? Do they not talk and think faster in the depot than they did in the stage-office?

Walden,
SOUNDS

Nothing can be more useful to a man than a determination not to be hurried.

Journal,
MARCH 22, 1842

Time is but the stream I go a-fishing in. I drink at it; but while I drink I see the sandy bottom and detect how shallow it is. Its thin current slides away, but eternity remains.

Walden,
WHERE I LIVED, AND WHAT I LIVED FOR

Above all, we cannot afford not to live in the present. He is blessed over all mortals who loses no moment of the passing life in remembering the past. Unless our philosophy hears the cock crow in every barnyard within our horizon, it is belated. That sound commonly reminds us that we are growing rusty and antique in our employments and habits of thought. His philosophy comes down to a more recent time than ours. There is something suggested by it that is a newer testament — the gospel according to this moment. He has not fallen astern; he has got up early and kept up early, and to be where he is is to be in season, in the foremost rank of time. It is an expression of the health and soundness of Nature, a brag for all the world, healthiness as of a spring burst forth, a new fountain of the Muses, to celebrate this last instant of time.

Walking

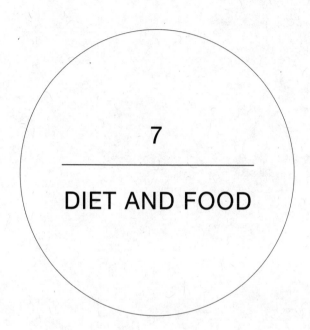

7

DIET AND FOOD

He will be regarded as a benefactor of his race who shall teach man to confine himself to a more innocent and wholesome diet. Whatever my own practice may be, I have no doubt that it is a part of the destiny of the human race, in its gradual improvement, to leave off eating animals, as surely as the savage tribes have left off eating each other when they came in contact with the more civilized.

Walden,
HIGHER LAWS

The repugnance to animal food is not the effect of experience, but is an instinct. It appeared more beautiful to live low and fare hard in many respects; and though

I never did so, I went far enough to please my imagination. I believe that every man who has ever been earnest to preserve his higher or poetic faculties in the best condition has been particularly inclined to abstain from animal food, and from much food of any kind. It is significant fact, stated by entomologists, I find it in Kirby and Spence, that "some insects in their perfect state, though furnished with organs of feeding, make no use of them"; and they lay it down as "a general rule, that almost all insects in this state eat much less than in that of larvae. The voracious caterpillar when transformed into a butterfly...and the gluttonous maggot when become a fly," content themselves with a drop or two of honey or some other sweet liquid. The abdomen under the wings of the butterfly still represents the larva. This is the tidbit which tempts his insectivorous fate. The gross feeder is a man in the larva state; and there are whole nations in that condition, nations without fancy or imagination, whose vast abdomens betray them.

Walden,
HIGHER LAWS

I learned from my two years' experience that it would cost incredibly little trouble to obtain one's necessary food, even in this latitude; that a man may use as simple a diet as the animals, and yet retain health and strength. I have made a satisfactory dinner, satisfactory on several accounts, simply off a dish of purslane (*Portulaca oleracea*) which I gathered in my cornfield, boiled and salted. I give the Latin on account of the savoriness of the trivial name. And pray what more can a reasonable man desire, in peaceful times, in ordinary noons, than a sufficient number of ears of green sweet-corn boiled, with the addition of salt? Even the little variety which I used was a yielding to the demands of appetite, and not of health. Yet men have come to such a pass that they frequently starve, not for want of necessaries, but for want of luxuries.

Walden,
ECONOMY

I made a study of the ancient and indispensable art of bread-making, consulting such authorities as offered, going back to the primitive days and first invention of

the unleavened kind, when from the wildness of nuts
and meats men first reached the mildness and refine-
ment of this diet, and traveling gradually down in my
studies through that accidental souring of the dough
which, it is supposed, taught the leavening process,
and through the various fermentations thereafter, till
I came to "good, sweet, wholesome bread," the staff
of life. Leaven, which some deem the soul of bread,
the *spiritus* which fills its cellular tissue, which is religiously preserved like the vestal fire — some precious
bottleful, I suppose, first brought over in the May-
flower, did the business for America, and its influence is still rising, swelling, spreading, in cerealian
billows over the land — this seed I regularly and
faithfully procured from the village, till at length one
morning I forgot the rules, and scalded my yeast; by
which accident I discovered that even this was not
indispensable — for my discoveries were not by the
synthetic but analytic process — and I have gladly
omitted it since, though most housewives earnestly
assured me that safe and wholesome bread without
yeast might not be, and elderly people prophesied a
speedy decay of the vital forces. Yet I find it not to

be an essential ingredient, and after going without it for a year am still in the land of the living; and I am glad to escape the trivialness of carrying a bottleful in my pocket, which would sometimes pop and discharge its contents to my discomfiture. It is simpler and more respectable to omit it. Man is an animal who more than any other can adapt himself to all climates and circumstances.

Walden,
ECONOMY

Finally, as for salt, that grossest of groceries, to obtain this might be a fit occasion for a visit to the seashore, or, if I did without it altogether, I should probably drink the less water. I do not learn that the Indians ever troubled themselves to go after it.

Walden,
ECONOMY

There is a certain class of unbelievers who sometimes ask me such questions as, if I think that I can live on vegetable food alone; and to strike at the root of the matter at once — for the root is faith — I am accustomed to answer such, that I can live on board nails. If they cannot understand that, they cannot understand much that I have to say. For my part, I am glad to hear of experiments of this kind being tried; as that a young man tried for a fortnight to live on hard, raw corn on the ear, using his teeth for all mortar. The squirrel tribe tried the same and succeeded. The human race is interested in these experiments, though a few old women who are incapacitated for them, or who own their thirds in mills, may be alarmed.

Walden,
ECONOMY

The customs of some savage nations might, perchance, be profitably imitated by us, for they at least go through the semblance of casting their slough annually; they have the idea of the thing, whether they have the reality or not. Would it not be well if we were to celebrate such a "busk," or "feast of first fruits," as Bartram describes to have been the custom of the Mucclasse Indians? "When a town celebrates the busk," says he, "having previously provided themselves with new clothes, new pots, pans, and other household utensils and furniture, they collect all their worn-out clothes and other despicable things, sweep and cleanse their houses, squares, and the whole town, of their filth, which with all the remaining grain and other old provisions they cast together into one common heap, and consume it with fire. After having taken medicine, and fasted for three days, all the fire in the town is extinguished. During this fast they abstain from the gratification of every appetite and passion whatever. A general amnesty is proclaimed; all malefactors may return to their town."

Walden,
Economy

"We must have our bread." But what is our bread? Is it baker's bread? Methinks it should be very *home-made* bread. What is our meat? Is it butcher's meat? What is that which we *must* have? Is that bread which we are now earning sweet? Is it not bread which has been suffered to sour, and then been sweetened with an alkali, which has undergone the vinous, the ace-tous, and sometimes the putrid fermentation, and then been whitened with vitriol? Is this the bread which we must have? Man must earn his bread by the sweat of his brow, truly, but also by the sweat of his brain within his brow. The body can feed the body only. I have tasted but little bread in my life. It has been mere grub and provender for the most part. Of bread that nourished the brain and the heart, scarcely any. There is absolutely none on the tables even of the rich.

Familiar Letters, THOREAU TO HARRISON BLAKE,
MAY 2, 1848

As I came home through the woods with my string of fish, trailing my pole, it being now quite dark, I caught a glimpse of a woodchuck stealing across my path, and felt a strange thrill of savage delight, and was strongly tempted to seize and devour him raw; not that I was hungry then, except for that wildness which he represented.

Walden,
HIGHER LAWS

I believe in the forest, and in the meadow, and in the night in which the corn grows. We require an infusion of hemlock, spruce or arbor-vitae in our tea. There is a difference between eating and drinking for strength and from mere gluttony. The Hottentots eagerly devour the marrow of the koodoo and other antelopes raw, as a matter of course. Some of our northern Indians eat raw the marrow of the Arctic reindeer, as well as various other parts, including the summits of the antlers, as long as they are soft. And herein, perchance, they have stolen a march on the cooks of Paris. They get what usually goes to feed the fire. This is probably better than stall-fed beef and slaughterhouse pork to make a man of. Give me a wildness whose glance no civilization can endure — as if we lived on the marrow of koodoos devoured raw.

Walking

One farmer says to me, "You cannot live on vegetable food solely, for it furnishes nothing to make bones with"; and so he religiously devotes a part of his day to supplying his system with the raw material of bones, walking all the while he talks behind his oxen, which, with vegetable-made bones, jerk him and his lumbering plough along in spite of every obstacle. Some things are really necessaries of life in some circles, the most helpless and diseased, which in others are luxuries merely, and in others still are entirely unknown.

Walden,
ECONOMY

8

ASPIRATION

I found in myself, and still find, an instinct toward a higher, or, as it is named, spiritual life, as do most men, and another toward a primitive rank and savage one, and I reverence them both. I love the wild not less than the good.

Walden,
HIGHER LAWS

Heaven is under our feet as well as over our heads.

Walden,
THE POND IN WINTER

The Universe is wider than our views of it....Be a Columbus to whole new continents and worlds within you, opening new channels, not of trade, but of thought.

Walden,
CONCLUSION

In proportion as our inward life fails, we go more constantly and desperately to the post office. You many depend on it, that the poor fellow who walks away with the greatest number of letters, proud of his extensive correspondence, has not heard from himself this long while.

Life Without Principle

We are accustomed to say in New England that few and fewer pigeons visit us every year. Our forests furnish no mast for them. So, it would seem, few and fewer thoughts visit each growing man from year to year, for the grove in our minds is laid waste....Our winged thoughts are turned to poultry. They no longer soar....

We hug the earth — how rarely we mount! Methinks we might elevate ourselves a little more. We might climb a tree, at least....

Walking

What a man thinks of himself, that it is which determines, or rather indicates, his fate....

But man's capacities have never been measured; nor are we to judge of what he can do by any precedents, so little has been tried.

Walden,
Economy

I know of no more encouraging fact than the unquestionable ability of man to elevate his life by a conscious endeavor.

Walden,
Where I Lived, and What I Lived For

If one advances confidently in the direction of his dreams, and endeavors to live the life which he has imagined, he will meet with a success unexpected in common hours....

If you have built castles in the air, your work need not be lost; that is where they should be. Now put the foundations under them.

Walden,
CONCLUSION

Goodness is the only investment that never fails.

Walden,
HIGHER LAWS

Why should we be in such desperate haste to succeed, and in such desperate enterprises? If a man does not keep pace with his companions, perhaps it is because he hears a different drummer. Let him step to the music which he hears, however measured or far away.

Walden,
CONCLUSION

I have met with but one or two persons in the course of my life who understood the art of Walking, that is, of taking walks — who had a genius, so to speak, for *sauntering*, which word is beautifully derived "from idle people who roved about the country, in the Middle Ages, and asked charity, under pretense of going a la Sainte Terre," to the Holy Land, till the children exclaimed, "There goes a Sainte-Terrer," a Saunterer, a Holy-Lander. They who never go to the Holy Land in their walks, as they pretend, are indeed mere idlers and vagabonds; but they who do go there are saunterers in the good sense, such as I mean. Some, however, would derive the word from sans terre, without land or a home, which, therefore, in the good sense, will mean, having no particular home, but equally at home everywhere. For this is the secret of successful sauntering. He who sits still in a house all the time may be the greatest vagrant of all; but the saunterer, in the good sense, is no more vagrant than the meandering river, which is all the while sedulously seeking the shortest course to the sea.

Walking

I think that we may safely trust a good deal more than we do. We may waive just so much care of ourselves as we honestly bestow elsewhere. Nature is as well adapted to our weakness as to our strength.

Walden,
ECONOMY

In the long run men hit only what they aim at. Therefore, though they fail immediately, they had better aim at something high.

Walden,
ECONOMY

No face which we can give to a matter will stead us so well at last as the truth. This alone wears well.

Walden,
CONCLUSION

To be a philosopher is not merely to have subtle thoughts, nor even to found a school, but so to love wisdom as to live, according to its dictates, a life of simplicity, independence, magnanimity, and trust. It is to solve some of the problems of life, not only theoretically, but practically.

Walden,
ECONOMY

I have always been regretting that I was not as wise as the day I was born.

Walden,
WHERE I LIVED, AND WHAT I LIVED FOR

No man ever followed his genius till it misled him.... If the day and the night are such that you greet them with joy, and life emits a fragrance like flowers and sweet-scented herbs, is more elastic, more starry, more immortal — that is your success....

Every man is the builder of a temple, called his body, to the god he worships, after a style purely his own, nor can he get off by hammering marble instead. We are all sculptors and painters, and our material is our own flesh and blood and bones. Any nobleness begins at once to refine a man's features, any meanness or sensuality to imbrute them.

Walden,
HIGHER LAWS

Rather than love, than money, than fame, give me truth. I sat at a table where were rich food and wine in abundance, and obsequious attendance, but sincerity and truth were not; and I went away hungry from the inhospitable board.... There was a man in my neighborhood who lived in a hollow tree. His manners were truly regal. I should have done better had I called on him.

Walden,
CONCLUSION

John Farmer sat at his door one September evening, after a hard day's work, his mind still running on his labor more or less.... He had not attended to the train of his thoughts long when he heard someone playing on a flute, and that sound harmonized with his mood.... The notes of the flute came home to his ears out of a different sphere from that he worked in, and suggested work for certain faculties which slumbered in him. They gently did away with the street, and the village, and the state in which he lived. A voice said to him, "Why do you stay here and live this mean moiling life, when a glorious existence is possible for you? Those same stars twinkle over other fields than these." But how to come out of this condition and actually migrate thither? All that he could think of was to practice some new austerity, to let his mind descend into his body and redeem it, and treat himself with ever increasing respect.

Walden,
Higher Laws

My desire for knowledge is intermittent, but my desire to bathe my head in atmospheres unknown to my feet is perennial and constant. The highest that we can attain to is not Knowledge, but Sympathy with Intelligence. I do not know that this higher knowledge amounts to anything more definite than a novel and grand surprise on a sudden revelation of the insufficiency of all that we called Knowledge before — a discovery that there are more things in heaven and earth than are dreamed of in our philosophy. It is the lighting up of the mist by the sun.

Walking

It is only when we forget all our learning that we begin to know. I do not get nearer by a hair's breath to any natural object so long as I presume that I have an introduction to it from some learned man. To conceive of it with a total apprehension I must for the thousandth time approach it as something totally strange. If you would make acquaintance with the ferns you must forget your botany. You must get rid of what is commonly called *knowledge* of them. Not a single scientific term or distinction is the least to the purpose, for you would fain perceive something, and you must approach the object totally unprejudiced. You must be aware that *no thing* is what you have taken it to be. In what book is this world and its beauty described? Who has plotted the steps toward the discovery of beauty? You have got to be in a different state from common. Your greatest success will be simply to perceive that such things are, and you will have no communication to make to the Royal Society.

Journal,
OCTOBER 4, 1859

The life in us is like the water in the river. It may rise this year higher than man has ever known it, and flood the parched uplands.... Only that day dawns to which we are awake. There is more day to dawn. The sun is but a morning star.

Walden,
CONCLUSION

BIBLIOGRAPHIC NOTES

The standard edition of Thoreau's complete works is the twenty-volume set published in 1906 by Houghton Mifflin. Thoreau's books, essays, and multivolume journal have been published in numerous editions and collections. Many biographies and collections of correspondence and criticism are also available. Below is a partial list of Thoreau's works, some of which were published posthumously.

BOOKS

A Week on the Concord and Merrimack Rivers, 1849
Walden; or, Life in the Woods, 1854
The Maine Woods, 1864

Cape Cod, 1865
A Yankee in Canada, 1866

ESSAYS

Paradise (to Be) Regained, 1843
On the Duty of Civil Disobedience, 1849
Slavery in Massachusetts, 1854
A Plea for Captain John Brown, 1860
Wild Apples, 1862
Walking, 1862
Life Without Principle, 1863

JOURNALS AND LETTERS

The Journal of Henry David Thoreau
The Writings of Henry David Thoreau:
Familiar Letters (edited by F. B. Sanborn)

ABOUT THE AUTHOR

Henry David Thoreau was born on July 12, 1817, in Concord, Massachusetts, where he lived for most of his life, except for brief sojourns out of state and to Canada. After attending college at Harvard, he returned home to Concord and supported himself in diverse ways — in the family pencil-making business and as handyman, teacher, lecturer, and surveyor.

On July 4, 1845, Thoreau decided to move to Walden Pond, on the outskirts of Concord, where he built a cabin in the woods, remaining there for a little over two years. He recounted his experience in essential living in *Walden; or, Life in the Woods*, published in 1854, seven years after he left Walden Pond.

Thoreau not only is one of the greatest American authors but commands a major place in world literature as well; his works have been translated into virtually every modern language. He wrote many books and essays, in addition to his voluminous journal, from which he drew much of the material for his other works. Thoreau died in Concord of tuberculosis on May 6, 1862.

ABOUT THE EDITOR

Carol Spenard LaRusso, formerly a senior editor at New World Library, has a BA and an MA in English literature. She taught English at San Francisco State University and piano at her home studio. Born and raised in New York, she lives in the wine country of Sonoma County, California, near her children and grandchildren.

Our products are available
in bookstores everywhere.
For our catalog, please contact:

New World Library
14 Pamaron Way
Novato, California 94949

Phone: 415-884-2100 or 800-972-6657
Catalog requests: Ext. 50
Orders: Ext. 52
Fax: 415-884-2199
Email: escort@newworldlibrary.com

To subscribe to our electronic newsletter, visit
www.newworldlibrary.com